OPRAH WINFREY

"I Don't Believe in Failure"

Robin Westen

Series Consultant:
Dr. Russell L. Adams, Chairman
Department of
Afro-American Studies,
Howard University

Enslow Publishers, Inc.

40 Industrial Road   PO Box 38
Box 398   Aldershot
Berkeley Heights, NJ 07922   Hants GU12 6BP
USA   UK

http://www.enslow.com

**"I DON'T BELIEVE IN FAILURE.
IT IS NOT FAILURE IF YOU ENJOYED THE PROCESS."**
—Oprah Winfrey

For Dr. Bebop and Gabriel Sky

Library of Congress Cataloging-in-Publication Data

Westen, Robin.
    Oprah Winfrey : "I don't believe in failure" / Robin Westen.
      p. cm. — (African-American biography library)
    Includes bibliographical references and index.
    ISBN 0-7660-2462-8
    1. Winfrey, Oprah—Juvenile literature. 2. Television personalities—United States—Biography—Juvenile literature. 3. African American television personalities—United States—Biography—Juvenile literature. 4. Actors—United States—Biography—Juvenile literature. 5. African American actors—United States—Biography—Juvenile literature. I. Title. II. Series.
PN1992.4.W56W47 2005
791.4502'8'092—dc22

                                2004016800

Printed in the United States of America

10 9 8 7 6 5 4 3 2

To Our Readers:
We have done our best to make sure all Internet Addresses in this book were active and appropriate when we went to press. However, the author and the publisher have no control over and assume no liability for the material available on those Internet sites or on other Web sites they may link to. Any comments or suggestions can be sent by e-mail to comments@enslow.com or to the address on the back cover.

Every effort has been made to locate all copyright holders of material used in this book. If any errors or omissions have occurred, corrections will be made in future editions of this book.

Illustration Credits: AP Photo/*The Plain Dealer*, Eustacio Humphrey, p. 107; AP/Wide World, pp. 3, 4, 8, 11, 48, 50, 56, 57, 59, 65, 68, 70, 73, 75, 81, 87, 93, 101, 102, 104, 111; Enslow Publishers, Inc., p. 91; Everett Collection, pp. 60, 78, 85, 98; Historic Photograph Collection of the Milwaukee Public Library, p. 22; Kosciusko Tourist Promotion Council, p. 19; Metropolitan Government Archives of Nashville and Davidson County, pp. 15, 34, 36, 38, 39, 40; Sara McIntosh Wooten, pp. 28, 32.

Cover Illustrations: AP/Wide World.

Contents

Chapter 1

"Okay, God, I Get It!"

tanding under the hot South African sun, Oprah Winfrey beams brightly. Winfrey, the wealthiest and most powerful American woman in the entertainment industry, is wearing an elegant dress, gold jewelry, and—a construction worker's hardhat. Standing beside her, also in a rugged hardhat, is the world-renowned civil rights activist and former president of South Africa, Nelson Mandela, along with the South African minister of education, Professor Kader Asmal, and several other respected dignitaries.

Winfrey gathers her strength, jabs a shovel into the ground, and scoops up a hefty mound of rich, dark earth. She tosses it into the air, and the press and spectators erupt into enthusiastic applause and resounding cheers.

It is December 6, 2002. Oprah Winfrey has just broken ground for the Oprah Winfrey Leadership Academy for Girls, a South African boarding school for grades seven through twelve. The new school will be devoted exclusively to 450 academically talented young women.

The academy, scheduled to open in 2007, holds a special place in Winfrey's heart. The Oprah Winfrey Foundation, an organization that was established to support the well-being of women, children, and families around the world, has already pledged $10 million to build and maintain the school.

Winfrey tells the crowd: "Education is the way to move mountains, to build bridges, to change the world. Education is the path to the future."

She adds, "I believe that education is indeed freedom. With God's help, these girls will be the future leaders on the path to peace in South Africa and the world."[1]

> "Education is the way to move mountains."

Winfrey's vision for the school includes classrooms that hold the latest in state-of-the-art technology, such as personal computers and well-equipped science laboratories. There will also be a fully stocked library with wall-to-wall books, an amphitheater designed for performances, and a gymnasium, as well as several sports fields, hundreds of dormitory rooms, and a vast dining room. The academy for girls will be built on twenty-two acres in Guateng Province, which is south of Johannesburg.

Winfrey is pouring her heart and soul into this project. She wants the school to embrace the young students in a nurturing and supportive environment. Winfrey is also focusing her attention on the educational programs, ensuring that they will be of the highest standards.

Even though Winfrey has an extremely hectic schedule back in the United States—with her enormously successful daily talk show, a busy production company that creates television programs as well as full-length movies, the cable network Oxygen, the national magazine called *O*, as well as numerous other philanthropic projects—she makes this promise: "I will be overseeing even the smallest details."[2]

Winfrey then gives an example of her commitment to the academy. "As

South Africa and the Policy of Apartheid

"Apartheid" literally means "apartness." Apartheid was the official policy of racial segregation and white supremacy enforced by the South African government for forty-six years. Its aim was to restrict the areas where nonwhites could live and to severely limit their governing power.

In 1994, after intense political struggles and much bloodshed, the African National Congress (ANC) came into power and officially ended apartheid. It was hoped that new nondiscriminatory policies would help relieve the widespread poverty of nonwhites in South Africa. But South Africa has lost 500,000 jobs in the past decade, and poverty continues to plague the country.

I sat down with my staff the other day and we were talking about the library, I said, 'There is no fireplace in the library. This is the girls' home. They need a fireplace in the wintertime to read.' So, we'll have a fireplace in the library. I believe we will make this school a home."[3]

Breaking ground for the academy was not Winfrey's only stop in South Africa that year. During the same Christmas season, she traveled throughout the country with thousands of boxes filled with clothing and toys for

With a shy smile, little Diong accepts a Christmas gift from Oprah Winfrey on her visit to his orphanage.

◆ ◆ ◆ ◆ ◆

more than fifty thousand orphans. Most of these children lost their parents because of the AIDS epidemic. Winfrey's gift giving was coined "Christmas Kindness South Africa 2002."

After her return, even though it was back to business as usual, Winfrey remained deeply moved by her experiences in South Africa. Her journey through the country, giving away gifts to AIDS orphans, was especially life-changing for Winfrey. Seeing the faces of the children and witnessing their joy was a contagious and powerful experience. "I realized . . . joy has a texture . . . if there's enough of it, you can feel it in the room. . . . I said in that moment, 'Okay, God, I get it!'"[4] Since that journey of discovery, Winfrey has not had a bad day, because, she says, "it puts everything in perspective."[5]

Thanks to her trip to Africa, Winfrey decided to use her influence to make the world aware of the seriousness of the AIDS crisis in South Africa. One devastating fact she cited is that 99 percent of AIDS-infected Africans are not able to get the drugs they need.

More than 13 million children under the age of fifteen living in a part of Africa known as the sub-Sahara have lost at least one parent to AIDS, and the number is growing. More than 90 percent of the world's orphans live in Africa.

In 2003, Winfrey visited South Africa again. This time she personally hosted 124 AIDS-infected children from

Soweto at a special celebration—an unforgettable Christmas party. As they arrived, the children walked down a red carpet and were welcomed with hugs and kisses.

This was especially powerful because sometimes people are afraid to touch children with AIDS. They mistakenly believe the disease is spread by casual contact.

Throughout the day, the children were treated to festivities including music and games and plenty of food. They were also given gifts of toys and shoes. For some of the children, who had lived for so long with nothing, the day was overwhelming. "One little girl was so excited that she could not open her present, and instead was kissing the plastic," said Winfrey.[6]

At the end of the party, the children received photos of themselves standing next to their famous host, Oprah Winfrey. "It was the best day of my life," Winfrey said, "just to see the joy on these kids' faces."[7]

Although Winfrey feels a special connection to South Africa, it is far from the only place she has cast her generous gaze, and it is hardly the first. It is estimated that since the late 1980s, the media mogul, who was born to a struggling single mother, grew up in poverty and hardship, and spent her early years in a small, rural farmhouse in Mississippi, has donated more than $50 million to charity.[8]

Winfrey has hopes for many future charitable endeavors. On her list are plans to help pay for the construction of additional schools in South Africa, as well as a school

Few experiences have been as life-changing for Winfrey as bringing food, clothing, books, and toys to tens of thousand of children in South Africa.

for girls in Afghanistan, where the Taliban, a strict Islamic military group that was in power in the country until 2002, had kept girls from attending school.

Winfrey also plans to produce a documentary about orphans throughout the world. The idea came to Winfrey during her trip to Africa, where she met children as young as nine years old who were taking care of their siblings after both parents had died of AIDS or other diseases.

To bring attention to this problem and do what she can

to change it, Winfrey also plans to bring in other charitable organizations so they can pool their efforts.

If the past points to the future, there is little doubt Oprah Winfrey will succeed. Obstacles never stood for very long in Winfrey's way when she was growing up. She learned as a child to meet life's challenges head-on—and to follow the light of her open heart and generosity.

Chapter 2

Born Into Hardship

n the early 1950s, the American South was still segregated. Blacks and whites were kept apart from one another in all aspects of society. They could not eat in the same restaurants or stay in the same hotels. On buses, white people sat upfront while black people had to ride in the back. But along the rolling hills of central Mississippi in the small town of Kosciusko, segregation did not hold tight with such a fierce grip. Kosciusko's former mayor Freddie George later described race relations in the small town during his time in office: "We existed together. We farmed together. We did business with each other."[1]

Still, Kosciusko lacked many educational and economic opportunities. Modern-day conveniences like indoor plumbing and telephones were still unavailable.[2] The majority of the town's children, regardless of race, grew up without much hope for a bright future.

It was there, on January 29, 1954, in a small wooden farmhouse, that Oprah Gail Winfrey was born, the great granddaughter of slaves who were freed after the Civil War. The same year as Oprah's birth, the U.S. Supreme Court declared segregation in public schools to be illegal, and a seed of hope for a better future for blacks was planted.

From the start, thanks to what might be considered a quirk of fate, Oprah's name was marked with attention. Her great aunt Ida had come up with the name *Orpah* after a little-known character in the Bible's Book of Ruth. But when the midwife wrote the baby's name down, she accidentally switched the letters *r* and *p*. "Oprah" ended up on the birth certificate.

Despite Oprah's stamp of originality, her early life was filled with the all too common problems of poverty. Her mother, Vernita Lee, was only eighteen years old when Oprah was born. Her father, Vernon Winfrey, was a twenty-year-old soldier stationed at Camp Rucker, a remote army base in Alabama. The teenagers hardly knew each other.

A few weeks after the birth, Vernon was surprised to receive a letter sent from Mississippi to his base. It was a printed announcement of Oprah's birth, along with a scrawled note written by Vernita asking him to "Send clothes!"[3] Vernon was not quick to help out with Oprah's care, though he later expressed regret about it.

Vernon Winfrey, Oprah's dad.

For the first few years, Oprah was raised by both her mother and her grandmother, Hattie Mae Lee. They did not have much money and shared a simple life. They lived together on a small farm in Kosciusko with cows, pigs, and chickens. Oprah ate the food that was grown on the farm and wore the clothes that her grandmother sewed for her.

When Oprah was four years old, her mother, Vernita, learned that there were housekeeping jobs in Milwaukee, a big city in Wisconsin, and the pay could be as high as $50 a week. This was considerably more money than the young mother could hope to earn in Kosciusko. It was too much to pass up.

Oprah's mother wanted to improve her life, so she became one of the almost 5 million African Americans who moved to northern cities between 1900 and 1960 hoping to find better lives. The movement was called the Great Migration. Vernita could not care for her small baby and work at the same time, so little Oprah was left with her grandmother.

Daily life on Hattie Mae Lee's rural farm was slow-paced yet rigorous. When Oprah was old enough, she had to help her grandmother with daily chores. Barefooted, she carried water from the well to the house, fed the chickens and pigs, and led the cows into the pasture.

The work was hard and steady, but there was still plenty of time left before the sun went down for Oprah to play. There were no other children to play with, and the nearest

The Great Migration

Between 1915 and 1920, almost one million African Americans moved from the rural South to the industrialized cities in the North and Midwest hoping to find employment and escape racism. In the decades that followed, almost a million more blacks moved west, especially to California. The trend of leaving small rural areas to settle in big cities continued, and by the 1960s, 40 percent of African Americans had left the South—and 75 percent of all African Americans were living in cities. As they settled into their urban homes, a new black culture was created.

neighbor was a blind man up the road. So little Oprah improvised. She spent her free time on the farm talking to the animals. Even as a small child, she had the gift of being able to carry on spontaneous conversations. "There weren't many kids . . . no play mates, no toys except for one corncob doll. I played with the animals and made speeches to the cows," she said.[4]

Hattie Mae loved Oprah, but like many adults during that time, she was a strict disciplinarian and believed it was in Oprah's best interests to tame her granddaughter's lively spirit. In those days, children were sometimes hit with tree branches called "switches" when they misbehaved. The heart-wrenching commands by Hattie Mae to go out into the field and pull down a branch to be used for her beating still burn uneasily in Oprah's memory. Oprah once said, "She could whip me for days and never get tired. It would be called child abuse now."[5]

Despite her grandmother's strict rules and harsh discipline, Oprah could feel Hattie Mae's love. Years later, Oprah expressed gratitude for her grandmother's strict upbringing. "I am what I am today because of my grandmother; my strength, my sense of reasoning, everything."[6]

Hattie Mae could also offer comfort to her granddaughter. Oprah remembers a time when her grandmother showed her fierce protective love. While they were lying in their shared featherbed, a thunderstorm raged outside. Hattie Mae held the trembling Oprah in her arms and reassured her with gentle words, "God doesn't mess with his children."[7]

A deeply religious woman, Hattie Mae made sure Oprah attended the Buffalo United Methodist Church every Sunday. The services lasted from morning until late afternoon, often in a room stifling with southern heat. Children had to sit quietly, with no fidgeting. It was not an easy task, especially for Oprah, a child filled with energy and curiosity.

Hattie Mae believed strongly in the importance of education. Even though she was not formally educated herself, she wanted Oprah to grow up reading the Bible. So when most three-year-olds were just learning to identify colors, Oprah was reading, adding, subtracting, writing, and putting Scripture to memory.

To Hattie Mae's delight, Oprah was able to memorize long passages from the Bible and other religious books. Proud of her granddaughter's accomplishments, she arranged for Oprah to speak at a church service on Easter Sunday.

The theme of Oprah's talk was "Jesus Rose on Easter Day." Her recitation was confident and flawless. It earned her the admiration of the parishioners. A woman sitting near the beaming Hattie Mae leaned over and remarked,

Here, at Buffalo United Methodist Church, three-year-old Oprah delighted everyone with her Easter speech. "The child is gifted," said one woman.

"The child is gifted."[8] Not surprisingly, Oprah's masterful ability to recite Scripture did not impress kids her own age. They often made fun of her serious church side, teasing and calling her "Little Preacher."

Oprah sensed she was different from the other children, a feeling heightened when in the autumn of 1959 she started kindergarten in nearby Buffalo, Mississippi. Since she could already read and write, she was bored in class and decided to do something about it. She wrote a letter to the teacher, saying, "Dear Miss New. I do not think I belong here."[9] Oprah's academic skill shone through the words in her letter. With the consent of the school administrator, Oprah was moved into the first grade.

Until then, the only life six-year-old Oprah had ever known was on her grandmother's rural farm. But reality for Oprah was about to change dramatically. When Hattie Mae became ill and could no longer care for her grandchild, Oprah was sent to live with her mother, Vernita Lee, in Milwaukee. Days in the rural South might have been lonely for Oprah, but life in the big city held its own trials.

Chapter 3

Tough Times

ustling Milwaukee, Wisconsin, an industrial
midwestern city, with crowds of hurrying
people, tall buildings, factories, and noisy
street traffic, was in stark contrast to the slow
pace of southern country life Oprah had always known.
Unfortunately, there would be no refuge for Oprah from
the city's hustle and bustle.

Oprah's new home turned out to be grim and unwel-
coming. It was only one dark and cramped room in a
run-down boardinghouse. Oprah was forced to share the
tiny downtown space with her mother and new half-sister,
Patricia. Oprah was given a narrow cot and had to sleep on
the porch, while her baby sister shared a bed with her
mother. Oprah said, "I felt like I was an outcast. I don't
know why my mother ever decided she wanted me. She
wasn't equipped to take care of me. I was just an extra
burden on her."[1]

Trying to make ends meet, Vernita worked all day long
as a maid. She had to travel long hours to and from the

Six-year-old Oprah found her world turned upside-down when she moved to the bustling city of Milwaukee.

◆ ◆ ◆ ◆ ◆

suburbs. Oprah was often left in the care of neighbors and distant relatives. When her mother came home at night, she was exhausted and could not find the strength to pay attention to Oprah.

Oprah wanted a pet to keep her company, but her mother, already overburdened in the cramped single room, would not allow it. Oprah, using her imagination, came up with a solution. She caught roaches, which were plentiful in the apartment. "I would name them and put them in a jar and feed them . . . like kids catching lightning bugs," she said.[2] She named two of her roaches Melinda and Sandy.

Oprah was growing into a strong-willed and outspoken child. She continued to excel in school, but she was not getting along with her mother. She was disobedient and disrespectful.

> Oprah's mother worked long hours and came home too tired to play with her daughter.

Eventually realizing that caring for Oprah was more than she could handle, Vernita contacted Vernon Winfrey, Oprah's father, and asked if their daughter could go live with him. When he agreed, she put Oprah on a bus to Nashville, Tennessee, where Vernon was living with his wife, Zelma.

When eight-year-old Oprah arrived in Nashville, her father was waiting for her at the station. At the time, little Oprah had no way of knowing the wonderful possibilities that awaited in her father's stable home.

Vernon and Zelma Winfrey lived in a modest house on the east side of Nashville. Vernon was a quiet man who worked hard and held down two jobs. At the time, he was a janitor at Vanderbilt University and worked in the kitchen at a Nashville hospital. The couple was childless and more than happy to welcome Oprah into their home.

Although the Winfreys were stern and did not show their love with spontaneous hugs and kisses, Oprah could

> At her father's house, Oprah's spiritual and academic growth were high priorities.

still feel the couple's devotion. They poured their energy into Oprah's spiritual and academic education, taking her to Baptist church on Sundays, drilling her on multiplication tables, insisting she read and write book reports, and quizzing her regularly on vocabulary words.

Soon after she arrived in Nashville, Vernon and Zelma took Oprah to the library and helped her get a library card. Having a library card gave Oprah a real feeling of community and helped to widen her horizons.[3]

Her fourth-grade teacher, Mary Duncan, also encouraged Oprah to use her mind. Miss Duncan nurtured Oprah's intelligence, urging her to read lots of books and enjoy being smart.

Like a flower that blooms in the sunshine, Oprah thrived in Nashville. But her happiness was not to last. When the school year came to a close and summer arrived, Vernita took Oprah back to Milwaukee.

A lot had changed while Oprah was gone. Her mother had moved into a two-room apartment and had given birth to another baby, Jeffrey. She was feeling hopeful about the future. "Come live with me. I'm gonna get married and we're all gonna be a real family," she promised Oprah.[4]

Despite Vernita's optimism, life in Milwaukee turned

out to be even more difficult for Oprah than before. Now she had to share a small apartment with her half-sister, Patricia, as well as Vernita's live-in boyfriend, and the baby, Jeffrey. She spent the long, hot summer reading and taking care of her sister or the new baby.

Oprah longed to be back with her father and Zelma, where she was the only child in the home and the focus of loving attention. But at summer's end, when Vernon came to get Oprah, Vernita refused to return the child. Saddened, Vernon had to return home without his daughter.

Oprah's life with her mother continued down a grim path. Vernita's crowded apartment served as a stopping ground for various relatives who stayed there when they had nowhere else to go. The door was open—and tragedy walked in.

One night when Oprah was nine years old, she was left alone with a cousin who was supposed to look after her. The nineteen-year-old boy raped her. Frightened and confused, Oprah kept it a secret. She was afraid that because she was only a child no one would believe her.[5]

Sadly, this was not an isolated incident. Sexual abuse continued through Oprah's adolescence. "It happened over a period of years, between nine and fourteen. It happened at my own

> For Oprah, going back to live with her mother led to trouble— and tragedy.

house, by different people—this man, that man, a cousin. . . . I remember blaming myself for it, thinking something must be wrong with me."[6]

Even though she had sexual experiences, Oprah remained innocent of the facts of life well into her early teens. It was only during a playground conversation at school that she finally learned how babies were made. Oprah was suddenly filled with fear. From then on, each time she felt sick to her stomach, she panicked, thinking she might be pregnant. It was this terror that Oprah later said was the hardest part of the abuse.

Stifling her anger and hurt, Oprah somehow managed to concentrate on her schoolwork. Her focus on academics opened what was to become a complex opportunity. While she was attending Lincoln Middle School in downtown Milwaukee, a teacher named Eugene Abrams observed her in the cafeteria. While all the other students were talking loudly and fooling around, Oprah sat all alone each day, completely absorbed in whatever book she was reading.

One of Oprah's middle-school teachers took a special interest in her education.

Impressed with Oprah's studiousness, Abrams suspected she had real potential to excel in the academic world. He spoke to Oprah's other teachers. They agreed Oprah was special.

With the best of intentions, Abrams nominated Oprah for a new program called Upward Bound. He wanted her to be able to attend school in a wealthier area, where she would have greater scholastic opportunities.

Thirteen-year-old Oprah was accepted with a full scholarship into Nicolet High, a privileged private school about twenty-five miles outside Milwaukee. While Nicolet was superior to her rough public school, the transition was fraught with difficulties for Oprah. She had to take three different buses each way to get to the new school. She was traveling from the inner city to the outer suburbs along with maids just like her mother.

Oprah was popular in her new school and frequently invited to the homes of her wealthy classmates. Many of the young girls offered their

Upward Bound

In June 1966, the U.S. government set up a national program called Upward Bound, which still exists today. Its purpose is to help students from disadvantaged homes continue on an educational path that will lead to college. The program serves students from low-income families and from families in which neither parent is college-educated. Upward Bound students are provided with information about scholarships and other financial-aid possibilities as well as counseling, mentoring, tutoring, exposure to cultural events, and enrollment in special academic programs. Since its start, an estimated 2 million Upward Bound students have graduated from college.

friendship, but Oprah could not help feeling different. The way her white classmates lived, with their spacious homes, stocked refrigerators, and enormous wardrobes, was in stark contrast to her own squalid life in the downtown Milwaukee apartment.

Oprah so wanted to fit in that she lied about her real situation. "I used to make up stories about my mother and my dad. I told the biggest lies about them because I wanted to be like everybody else."[7]

Of the two thousand students at Nicolet High School, Oprah was the only African American.

Meanwhile, her mother, Vernita, was struggling just to make ends meet. There was no money left in the family budget for any extras. Oprah wanted to play tennis, go to the movies, or share a pizza, the kinds of activities her private-school friends took for granted. Yearning to be like everyone else in her school, Oprah started stealing money from her mother's purse.

> Oprah started stealing money from her mother's purse.

Fueled by the smoldering anger over the sexual abuse and by the chaos in her living situation, Oprah's rebellion turned into a self-destructive wildfire. Her acting out escalated. Oprah stayed out late, had sexual encounters with boys, and talked back to her mother. She told lies, one on top of another. "I caused all kinds of problems for myself," Oprah said later.[8] Rather than face the consequences for her bad behavior, she ran away again and again. Anxious to gain some control over her daughter's behavior, Vernita decided to send Oprah to a halfway house for troubled teenage girls. As luck would have it, the home was already overcrowded, and there was no room for Oprah. Vernita loved her daughter but understood that she could not give her the attention and strict discipline she desperately needed.

Vernita knew what she had to do: She had no choice but to return Oprah to her father and Zelma's home in Nashville. Oprah left Milwaukee carrying not only her suitcases—but a secret too heavy to carry.

Chapter 4

Beating the Odds

Vernon and Zelma were delighted to have Oprah back in their home, though she was a changed girl from the nine-year-old they had last seen. Now thirteen years old, Oprah was a sassy teenager who strutted around in suggestive clothing. She was rude to Vernon, calling him by the disrespectful name "Pops."

Oprah's tough-as-nails attitude was covering up a powerful secret she would not be able to hide for much longer. She was seven months pregnant. Oprah knew that before long she would have to confess her condition to her father. But on the very same day she got up the nerve to tell him, the baby was born. Sadly, a few days later, the newborn died.

Oprah was shaken by the chain of life-changing events. "I went back to school after the baby died, thinking that I had been given a second chance in life. I threw myself into books. I read books about troubled women, Helen Keller and Anne Frank."[1]

Vernon's strong words of encouragement and stern discipline coaxed Oprah into putting her past behind her. Oprah trusted that her Dad could help her straighten out her life because he was so clear

> Oprah's tough-as-nails attitude was covering up a powerful secret.

about what he expected of her. "Listen, girl, if I tell you a mosquito can pull a wagon," Vernon told her, "don't ask me no questions. Just hitch him up."[2]

Vernon now worked as a barber and owned a grocery store. He worked long hours, but that did not stop him from devoting himself to Oprah. One thing was for sure, neither Vernon nor Zelma was willing to put up with any more bad behavior. They set down strict rules, insisting that Oprah dress modestly and warning that she would suffer consequences if she talked back or disobeyed the rules. "I knew exactly what I could and what I couldn't get away with," Oprah said. "I *respected* his authority."[3] Vernon would warn his daughter, "Be home by midnight, or by God sleep on the porch!"[4]

Vernon and Zelma insisted that Oprah concentrate on her studies. Even though it was summertime, she had to learn at least five new vocabulary words each day and read several books a month. She also had to write reports about

Oprah's father was never too busy with his barbershop
and general store to keep a strict eye on his wild daughter.

the books, just as she had done the first time she lived with
them.

Instead of feeling oppressed by their tough love,
Oprah flourished. In September 1968, when Oprah was
fourteen, she started tenth grade at Nashville's East High
School. Unlike the private school in Milwaukee, where
Oprah was propelled by envy and where she always felt
different, the Nashville school was a perfect match. It was
an integrated environment, and there were plenty of middle-
class black students.

BEATING THE ODDS

Even so, Oprah had a slow academic start. Still reeling from the baby's death, coupled with the adjustment of starting a new school, Oprah at first managed only C's. Vernon insisted that his daughter try harder. He used powerful words to spur her on. "If you were a child who could only get C's, then that is all I would expect of you," he told her. "But you are not. And so in this house, for you, C's are not acceptable."[5]

Vernon and Zelma also put her on a new stricter schedule, which limited television watching. Vernon told her there were three kinds of people: "There are those who make things happen. There are those who watch things happen, and there are those that don't know what's happening."[6]

Oprah began to thrive under her father and Zelma's caring tutelage. Her academic career took off like a rocket. Before long, she was not only on the honor roll but also winning the respect of her teachers and fellow students and getting involved in extracurricular activities.

Oprah joined the drama club and practiced recitation and public speaking on the forensics team, a combination speech and debate team that traveled to other schools for competitions. Proud of her roots, Oprah spoke about famous antislavery activists Harriet Tubman and Sojourner Truth. She also gave readings

Oprah began to thrive in her father and Zelma's strict but loving care.

Oprah, center front, was elected vice president of the student council.

◆ ◆ ◆ ◆ ◆

from one of her most cherished books, Margaret Walker's *Jubilee*. The book tells the life story of Vyry, the daughter of a house slave and plantation owner.

By her senior year, buoyed by her increasing self-confidence, Oprah decided to run for vice president of the student council. Her down-to-earth promises appealed to her fellow classmates: better food in the cafeteria, greater school spirit, and a live band at the prom. The votes were counted, and Oprah won.

Based on her high grades and extracurricular activities, Oprah was invited that year to attend the White House Conference on Youth in Estes Park, Colorado. Along with exceptional students from all over the country and five hundred business leaders, she joined in a dialogue about issues that concerned teenagers. When she got back to Nashville, Oprah was interviewed by disc jockey John Heidelberg at a local African-American radio station, WVOL.

Meanwhile, Oprah continued to do well in school. This time her accomplishments did not set her apart from her classmates. Instead, her enthusiasm and focus won her the respect of her classmates, and her popularity grew even stronger. In 1971, while in her senior year, she threw a huge party to celebrate her seventeenth birthday. It had to be held in the school gym to make room for all her friends—she invited *everyone* in the school.

A few months later, Oprah got a phone call from John Heidelberg, the disc jockey who had interviewed her months earlier about the youth conference in Colorado. Recalling how well the high school student had spoken during their on-air interview, he asked Oprah to represent the radio station in the Miss Fire Prevention Contest in Nashville.

Vernon Winfrey was opposed to the idea, and Oprah did not at first agree to enter. She knew the competition would be fierce, with many beautiful young women vying for the title. But after mulling it over, Oprah decided she had nothing to lose and entered the contest.

When Oprah stood before the judges in her evening gown, she was the only black woman among a bevy of white women with fire engine red hair. Figuring she had no chance to win, Oprah was able just to relax and be herself during the competition. This relaxed attitude turned out to be a winning strategy.

When the judges asked each of the girls what they

Who would win the title of Miss Fire Prevention 1971?
Did Oprah, center, have a chance?

would do if they had a million dollars, Oprah's totally honest answer made them laugh out loud. "I would be a spendin' fool. I'm not quite sure what I would spend it on, but I would spend, spend, spend."[7]

When the questions turned more serious and Oprah was asked what she wanted to be when she was out in the world, her answer impressed them even more. "I said I wanted to be a broadcast journalist because I believed in the truth. I was interested in proclaiming the truth to the world."[8]

Oprah's humor, intelligence, and confident personality won the judges' votes. When she was crowned Miss Fire Prevention of 1971, Oprah became the first African-American woman to hold the title.

A few months later, Oprah went to WVOL, the radio station that had sponsored her in the pageant. She was there to collect a donation for the March of Dimes, a charitable organization that funds research to prevent birth defects. While she was there, the disc jockey, Heidelberg, handed her a paper and asked her to read into the microphone. He taped it and later played it for the station manager, Clarene Kilcrese. Impressed by Oprah's natural ability to speak on-air, Kilcrese offered her an after-school job reading the news on the radio.

> "I would be a spendin' fool. I'm not quite sure what I would spend it on, but I would spend, spend, spend."

The first ever African-American Miss Fire Prevention
waves to the crowd during her victory ride.

Now, instead of working in her father's grocery store
after school, she was reading the news every half hour
from four in the afternoon until eight-thirty in the
evening. Oprah was only seventeen years old, yet she had
landed her first on-air broadcast job and was earning $100
a week. This was a lot of money for a teenager.

Despite her busy senior year, Oprah managed to keep
up her grades while she worked at the radio station. Her
popularity in school also continued to spiral upward. She

was voted Most Popular Girl in her class and was dating the boy voted Most Popular, Anthony Otey. He was an honor student just like Oprah, and they were both members of the forensics team. Together, along with other classmates interested in public speaking, they would debate other schools.

Also in 1971, Oprah made her first trip to Los Angeles to give a speech. It was paid for by a church group. While there, Oprah visited the usual Hollywood tourist attractions.

Voted "Most Popular" at Nashville's East High School were Oprah and her boyfriend, Anthony Otey.

When she set foot on the sidewalk outside Grauman's Chinese Theatre, called the Hollywood Walk of Stars, she had a premonition. When she came back to Nashville, she told her father that one day her name, too, would be etched in concrete.

In the three years since Oprah had returned to her father's house, she had emerged from her earlier difficulties and focused on success. She won academic honors in high school, became a star on her school's debating team, earned the respect of her teachers and classmates, won a beauty pageant, and worked after school as a newscaster on an African-American radio station.

Oprah enjoyed her busy, happy senior year at Nashville's East High School.

Vernon was proud of all his daughter's accomplishments. Still, when it was time for Oprah to graduate and go to college, he did not feel she was ready to leave his watchful eye. He refused to let her attend a university away from home. Respectful of her father's wishes, Oprah registered at Tennessee State University (TSU), an all-black college not far from her Nashville home.

Oprah wanted to study television and radio, but TSU did not have a communications department. Instead, she majored in speech and drama. Around this time, a lot was happening on college campuses across the country. It was a time of upheaval. Many African-American students felt that society treated them unfairly. Hundreds of them joined a group called the Black Panthers. They wanted to raise black consciousness and were willing to use militant, even violent tactics, to reach their goals.

> Oprah did not share the anger and militancy that were felt by many other African-American students in the early 1970s.

Their militant philosophy did not fit in with Oprah's view of the world. Although she felt pride in her heritage, she was not angry. She did not feel as though she had experienced discrimination. This set her apart from many of the other students. She said her college classmates "resented me. I refused to conform to the militant thinking of the time."[9]

Oprah focused on her work in the drama department. In one memorable production, she played Coretta Scott King, wife of Martin Luther King, Jr.

While a freshman in college, Oprah entered the Miss Black Nashville Pageant, sponsored by the Negro Elks Club. She won the votes of judges not only for her poise and beauty but for her polished dramatic readings. As winner of the pageant, Oprah was qualified to run for Miss Black Tennessee.

Six other black women, also pageant winners, entered the competition. Oprah was certain any one of the other contestants, with classic beauty and light skin, would win the title. "I was raised to believe that the lighter your skin, the better you were," she once said.[10] To her astonishment, the judges voted for Oprah. The prize was scholarship money to go toward her college education.

Oprah continued to steer clear of the political climate on college campuses. But the tumultuous times of the late sixties and early seventies had paved the way for changes in government policy. The racial upheaval spearheaded by college students led to greater opportunities for African Americans in both educational institutions and the workplace.

The new government policy, called Affirmative Action, encouraged businesses to support its goals by offering financial incentives for hiring minorities, including women. Oprah had not joined the protesters who had worked toward change, but she was about to benefit from their activism.

Chapter 5

Changing Channels

When an executive at the WTVF station in Nashville heard Winfrey reading the news over the radio, he thought the young college student could fulfill two Affirmative Action requirements at the same time. After all, she was African American *and* a woman. He set up an audition.

Winfrey, still a college sophomore, was nervous. Although she was comfortable speaking into a radio microphone, she had never performed on camera before. Rather than just be herself, Winfrey decided to emulate Barbara Walters, the famous female newscaster and one of her idols. Winfrey crossed her legs just like Walters and also tried to imitate her speech patterns.[1]

This time Winfrey's tactic worked, and she was hired. But she did not harbor any illusions about why the station had given her such a prestigious position. She knew they did it as a way to conform to the Affirmative Action guidelines. Later, she reflected on the opportunity. "Sure, I was a token," she said. Winfrey meant she was hired just because she was a black woman—not necessarily because

Affirmative Action

In 1964 the United States set up the Affirmative Action policy. Its purpose was to compensate for decades-long discrimination against minorities and women. Schools and businesses receiving federal funds would have to admit a certain number of minority students into their schools, or hire a certain number minority employees in their companies. If not, they would lose their federal funding. This was called a quota system. In 1972 the Equal Employment Opportunities Act formed a commission to enforce the policy. However, by the late 1970s some people who were not members of a minority claimed that Affirmative Action quotas were creating reverse discrimination. Between 1979 and 1991, several cases were argued in the Supreme Court against the quota system. By 2003 the Court ruled that educational institutions could continue to consider race as a factor in admitting students as long as they did not set a specific quota.

of her gifts as a newscaster. Then she added. "But I was one *happy* token."[2]

In 1976, Winfrey's life was filled with sparkling possibilities. She was originally hired to work only on weekends, but Chris Clark, the news director at the station, took Winfrey under his wing and promoted her. She was now on the air every night, co-anchoring with a seasoned broadcaster, Harry Chapman.

This busy work schedule did not interfere with Winfrey's college education. She was poised to graduate, with only a senior project left to complete at TSU, when a hard-to-resist job opportunity came her way. She would have to decide whether to finish college or climb the next rung on the career ladder.

Radio station WJZ-TV in Baltimore, Maryland, the tenth largest broadcasting market in the nation, was scouting around for a new talent. They saw Winfrey on the

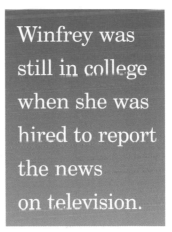

Winfrey was still in college when she was hired to report the news on television.

Nashville station and contacted her about a job. Even though it meant leaving college before officially graduating, Winfrey decided to take the ABC affiliate up on its offer.

In Winfrey's mind, it was the perfect time to leave Nashville. She had already gained experience working as a television anchor. Plus, she decided it was time to break free of her father's tight reins. Winfrey felt ready to enter adulthood. She wanted to take a chance in Baltimore and make a name for herself there.

Baltimore is a city on the East Coast with a more sophisticated, cultured, and quick-paced feel than Nashville. After Winfrey agreed to make the move, the station plastered the city with billboards reading WHAT'S AN OPRAH? as a way to heighten the audience's anticipation of her arrival. Although she was intimidated by the attention, it appears to have triggered Winfrey's innate determination.

> Oprah felt ready to break free of her father's tight reins.

Despite her high hopes, twenty-two-year-old Winfrey did not take easily to the new city. It took her more than a year to like living in Baltimore. "The first time I saw the downtown area I got so depressed that I called my daddy in Nashville and burst into tears," she said.[3]

Winfrey had to meet new challenges at her prestigious job. Every weekday night she sat beside Jerry Turner, a seasoned television reporter who had been anchoring the news in Baltimore for more than a decade. While he projected a professional delivery, Winfrey often got emotionally involved while delivering the news, occasionally crying over tragic stories.

Soon the television executives realized that the co-anchoring team was not working: Winfrey was not right for the on-air news job. They tried her out as an on-location reporter, but that did not work either. "My openness is the reason why I did not do so well as a news reporter . . . ," Winfrey said. "I used to go on assignment and be so open that I would say to people at fires and they've lost their children—'That's okay. You don't have to talk to me.'"[4]

Her personal and understanding approach did not please the television executives, but they had already signed Winfrey to a two-year contract. "I was devastated because up until that point, I had sort of cruised," she said.[5] Up until then, Winfrey's career path had been an easy slide to success.

On top of it, they insisted that Winfrey get a makeover. The executives sent her to New York City to get her hair styled. They did not want her wearing her natural Afro, which was a popular look at the time.

The new hairstyle was disastrous. The harsh chemicals meant to straighten her hair were kept on too long, and most of Winfrey's hair fell out. For months afterward, she had to wear a wig, which did little to help bolster her self-confidence. Winfrey said the incident helped her learn to appreciate herself for other qualities besides her looks.

Around the same time, when loneliness and disappointment seemed to be her only companions, Winfrey made a new friend, Gayle King. She was a production assistant at WJZ-TV. On the night of a fierce snowstorm, Winfrey invited Gayle, who lived thirty-five miles away from the station, to stay overnight at her house. Winfrey's apartment

Winfrey's openness and empathy spelled disaster for a newscaster, but they were the perfect qualities for a talk show host.

was closer to the station. The two women became quick friends, staying up and talking until dawn.[6]

They have been best friends ever since and speak on the phone every night. Winfrey said, "In spite of all the things that have happened to me, we laugh every night about one thing or another. She absolutely keeps me grounded."[7]

When spring arrived, the network hired a new general manager, Bill Baker. One of his jobs was to create a local show that could compete with a highly successful national talk show, *The Donahue Show*, hosted by Phil Donahue. Baker developed a show called *People Are Talking* and asked Winfrey to co-host it with Richard Sher. They were going to interview famous celebrities as well as ordinary people with newsworthy or human-interest stories to share.

People Are Talking turned out to be a perfect fit. Winfrey knew she had found her niche. "The minute the first show was over, I thought, 'Thank God, I've found what I was meant to do.' It's like breathing to me."[8] Ratings proved Winfrey right on target. They skyrocketed, and the network had a runaway hit. Women viewers in Baltimore were tuning into *People Are Talking* over the perennially popular *Donahue Show*.

Winfrey's first ratings surge over Phil Donahue brought her satisfaction. "I like Phil Donahue," she said. "But I have to

> "Thank God, I've found what I was meant to do. It's like breathing to me."

Gayle King, above, and Oprah quickly became best friends.

admit it feels good to beat him. For the longest time, I couldn't go about doing my job without people saying, *Yeah, you're good. But are you as good as Donahue?*"[9]

As a talk show host, Winfrey was a shining success, but at the same time her personal life was suffering. She had been involved in a relationship for four years.[10] In 1981, when it broke up, Winfrey was heartbroken. She called in sick to work for three straight days and then wrote a suicide note to her friend Gayle. She never gave the note to

Daytime Talk Shows

The earliest television talk shows shared many similarities with radio call-in programs. The first daytime talk show debuted on January 14, 1952, on NBC-TV. It was called the *Today Show* and was hosted by Dave Garroway, a former radio personality. Phil Donahue ran a radio call-in talk show, too, in Dayton, Ohio, before becoming the host of *The Donahue Show*. Donahue's television show debuted locally in Baltimore in 1967 and aired nationally from 1970 to 1996. He strongly encouraged audience participation by bounding around the studio with microphone in hand. Donahue's show often delved into offensive topics. When Winfrey rose to national syndication success in 1986, she followed Donahue's lead and aired what some critics called "trash" television.

her friend, nor did Winfrey attempt to kill herself. Years later, when speaking to reporters about this difficult time, Winfrey said the note was not serious. Yet undeniably, this was a period of emotional turmoil in her life.

Winfrey dealt with her pain by overeating. She looked to food to make her feel better and fill her empty heart. As a result, Winfrey gained more than fifty pounds. "Food meant security and comfort. Food meant love," Winfrey said.[11]

Despite her burgeoning weight, with the same determination that helped Winfrey transcend the consequences of her difficult childhood, she pulled herself out of despair and looked to the future. It was time to move on.

Chapter 6

In Her Own Name

t was the fall of 1984, and thirty-year-old Winfrey had been in Baltimore for six years co-hosting the town's top-rated talk show. Now she was more than eager for a change, looking forward to spreading her wings and putting real distance between herself and her failed relationship. Winfrey wanted to take on a bigger challenge.[1] When she heard about an opening at WLS-Television in the big city of Chicago, Illinois, for a show called *A.M. Chicago*, Winfrey was more than ready to try out for the job.

Chicago is nicknamed the "Windy City" because of forceful gale winds that blow off Lake Michigan during the winter months. It was also the city where the popular Phil Donahue show was produced. But harsh weather and fierce competition did not deter Winfrey. She knew this was a huge opportunity, and she flew to Chicago on Labor Day for an interview.

Winfrey took to Chicago's hustle and bustle the moment she arrived: "I set foot in this city and just walking down the street, it was like roots, like the motherland. I knew I belonged here," she said.[2]

When Winfrey got to WLS, rather than recite a prepared speech on her audition tape, she just chatted spontaneously, talking about her life and a host of other topics. As the station manager, Dennis Swanson, reviewed the tape, he was instantly impressed with her ease and confidence. He offered Winfrey the job that afternoon.

Winfrey wanted the prestigious position as host of the morning talk show, but she would not accept it unconditionally. She remembered what had happened in the past when television executives tried to change her image with a radical makeover. The results had been disastrous, and she was afraid she was in for the same treatment.

She made it clear to Swanson that she would not do anything drastic to change the way she looked. In the post-audition meeting, Dennis Swanson said he was more then pleased but was worried about one thing.

"I'll lose weight," Winfrey immediately said.

"No," Swanson replied. "Stay as you are. I'm only worried about how you will handle being famous."[3] These were exactly the words Winfrey wanted to hear.

At first, media experts did not agree with Swanson's upbeat appraisal of Winfrey's appeal. In fact, they thought she did not have a chance in big-time broadcasting, especially against the impressive Donahue. How could an overweight, practically unknown African-American woman be successful on Donahue's finely groomed home turf?

The handsome Donahue, with his crop of snow-white hair, had been hosting his popular daytime talk show for sixteen years. He had a mature, thought-provoking style that attracted housewives across America.

> "Stay as you are. I'm only worried about how you will handle being famous."

Yet it was not long before Winfrey proved the naysayers wrong and Swanson right. She was an almost instant hit. In only four weeks, she took the show from last place to first in its time slot. *The Donahue Show* was suddenly holding second place, and media experts quickly changed their tune.

One year later, thanks to her soaring ratings, *A.M. Chicago* was renamed *The Oprah Winfrey Show*. The next year, the show began to broadcast nationally, with at least 135 stations across the country airing it.

Not only did Winfrey get a television show in her name, but the Chicago station also gave her a huge raise. She began to donate large sums of money to charity, a practice that Winfrey would continue throughout her career.

**Phil Donahue had the number-one television talk show—
until Oprah Winfrey came along.**

One of the first projects Winfrey supported was the creation of a Big Sister group. She encouraged several female members of the show's staff to act as mentors to two dozen girls from a low-income housing project in Chicago. They met regularly, sometimes going to the library, other times to see movies or shopping together.

Winfrey wanted to help these girls develop healthy self-esteem so they would avoid teenage pregnancy, concentrate on their schoolwork, graduate, and succeed in life. She was generous with her time and money, but she was tough, too. She cautioned them: "Don't tell me you want to do great things with your life and still not be able to tell a boy no. You want something to love and to hug? Tell me and I'll get you a puppy!"[4]

Winfrey was also realistic about helping the girls. Because of her own childhood, she knew how hard they would have to struggle to overcome their hardships. By her own estimation, she thought it would be lucky if two

Television executives Roger King, left, and Joseph Ahern were happy to join Winfrey in announcing that *The Oprah Winfrey Show* would be broadcast all over the nation.

Maya Angelou

An African-American poet and author, Maya Angelou was born in 1928. She is known not only as a writer but also as a tireless civil rights activist. As early as 1959, Angelou worked with Martin Luther King, Jr. In the mid-sixties she edited several newspapers in Africa, including *The African Review* and *The Arab Observer*. Angelou is best known for her autobiographical works such as *I Know Why the Caged Bird Sings* and *All God's Children Need Traveling Shoes*. Her book *Just Give Me a Cool Drink of Water 'Fore I Die* was nominated for a Pulitzer Prize in 1991. Angelou read one of her poems, "On the Pulse of the Morning," at President Bill Clinton's inauguration in 1993.

out of the twenty-four girls could beat the odds.[5]

Being able to help others was one of the perks of Winfrey's high-profile job. Another was mingling with celebrities. With her trademark ease and enthusiasm, she interviewed celebrities including the ex-Beatle Paul McCartney; veteran actress Sally Field; famous Motown musician Stevie Wonder; TV star Candice Bergen; and supermodel Christie Brinkley. She even interviewed her mentors: television news anchor Barbara Walters and the African-American writer Maya Angelou.

Winfrey and Angelou quickly became good friends, and their friendship grew stronger in the years that followed.

But there was not always an upbeat atmosphere on

After Maya Angelou, above, appeared on Winfrey's show,
their lifelong friendship took root and began to grow.

Winfrey's shows. She also tackled serious issues and interviewed controversial guests. In 1985 she spoke with women who were members of the racist group the Ku Klux Klan (KKK). The women appeared on the show wearing the disturbing white robes and pointed hats of the KKK. Even though the group is known for its hatred of blacks, Jews, and other minorities, Winfrey stayed composed during the show. Later, though, she decided that

As Winfrey laughed and cried along with her studio audience, her popularity soared.

she did not want to let racists air their views on her talk show in the future.

Winfrey also interviewed ordinary people who had emotional stories to share. This gave her audience a chance to gain deeper insights into their own lives. Because her reactions were emotionally honest, they were sometimes surprising. Remembering her own tumultuous teen years, Winfrey was capable of losing patience and scolding a runaway teen appearing on her show for not taking control of her life.

Unlike Donahue, who had an intellectual approach, Winfrey reacted emotionally. At the station in Nashville, this had been seen as a handicap, but now it worked to her benefit. Winfrey could laugh and cry along with her guests, and the more honest and open she was, the more her popularity grew. When asked the reasons she thought this was so, she once said, "I think the reason why I work as well as I do on the air is that people sense the realness."[6]

On camera, Winfrey appeared relaxed and confident, but when she went home, the pressures of the day caught up with her. Rather than deal with the stress, she reverted to her old habit of turning to food as a way to calm her nerves. Within six months, she had gained more than twenty pounds. "I used to brag, 'I don't ever get stress,'" she said later. "The reason I didn't get stressed is, I ate my way through it."[7]

Although Winfrey's weight was the focus of cruel headline stories in national tabloids—the newspapers that specialize in sensational celebrity gossip—her size did not hurt her ratings or her chance to grow in other areas of the entertainment industry.

On the eve of her thirty-first birthday, Winfrey made a national appearance on the popular late-night talk show *The Tonight Show*, which was then hosted by Johnny Carson. This was the first time Winfrey was seen across the country and not just in the cities where her show was syndicated.

As it turned out, that very night Quincy Jones, the record producer and musician, was also a guest. Nothing eventful happened on the show that evening, but Jones would see Winfrey again—and that coincidence would lead Winfrey on an exciting new career path.

Chapter 7

A Passion
for Purple

n the winter of 1985, Quincy Jones was in Chicago on a brief business trip. While in his hotel room, he turned on the television set and absentmindedly flipped through the channels. Suddenly, he stopped short and fixed his gaze. Winfrey's morning talk show was on. A light went off in Jones's mind. Winfrey would be perfect for the role of Sofia in *The Color Purple*, a movie he was producing with Steven Spielberg. It was based on Alice Walker's best-selling book.

Jones did not know that Winfrey was already a huge admirer of Walker's book. A year before, she had read a review of *The Color Purple* in *The New York Times* and asked her local bookstore to put in an order for the book right away. When it arrived, she read it eagerly. It became one of her favorite books. So impressed was she with the novel, she bought several copies to give to her closest friends as gifts. "It was all I talked about for two years," she said.[1]

Winfrey was not alone in her admiration. *The Color Purple* went on to win the Pulitzer Prize for Fiction and has been translated into more than twenty languages. It has sold millions of copies all over the world.

When Winfrey first read the book, she identified strongly with Sofia, the same character Jones had in mind for her to play in the film. Sofia is a woman who, like Winfrey, refuses to let the hardships of her life destroy

The Pulitzer Prize

Every year since 1917, the Pulitzer Prize has been awarded for extraordinary contributions in arts and letters and journalism. A special board decides who will receive the awards, which are given out by the Columbia University Graduate School of Journalism, a respected school in New York City. The Pulitzer Prize was established by Joseph Pulitzer, a Hungarian-American journalist and newspaper publisher. Some famous people who have won a Pulitzer Prize include playwright Tennessee Williams, poet Robert Frost, novelist Alice Walker, and former president John F. Kennedy, who was honored for his book *Profiles in Courage*. The name *Pulitzer* is often mispronounced. The correct way to say it is "Pull it, sir."

With a national television show and an upcoming movie debut,
Winfrey was enjoying her success.

her spirit. Even though Sofia is abused by her husband, Harpo (coincidentally, Oprah spelled backward), and caught in a web of injustice, she remains passionately strong and outspoken. Like Winfrey, the fictional Sofia shares her personal wisdom with others.

A week after Quincy Jones returned to Los Angeles, his office called Winfrey to ask if she wanted to audition for the role. Winfrey packed her suitcase and flew to the West Coast studio. She was ready to face the challenge.

Her philosophy—always to walk toward opportunity when the door opens—gave Winfrey the confidence to try out for the part. "I believe that you tend to create your own blessings. You have to prepare yourself so that when opportunity comes, you're ready."[2]

Steven Spielberg called Winfrey into his office after viewing the audition tape and told her he was impressed with her acting ability. But he also cautioned Winfrey that he needed to audition other actresses before making a final decision.

Winfrey flew back to Chicago hopeful, but focused on the matters at hand. She still had a television talk show to host and a weight problem to deal with. She was still using food to deal with stress. To get a jump-start on a diet, Winfrey checked into a health farm—a

> "You have to prepare yourself so that when opportunity comes, you're ready."

retreat dedicated to helping clients lose weight and improve their well-being—to try to take off the extra pounds.

While there, she got an exciting phone call from the casting agent of *The Color Purple*. She had been chosen to play Sofia. The casting agent explained that one of the reasons Winfrey was chosen for the part was because of her physical appearance; her weight was perfect. The casting executive told her to leave the health facility right away and gain back the pounds she had lost before showing up on the film set.

The movie was made during eight weeks of shooting in South Carolina. Winfrey co-starred with Whoopi Goldberg and Danny Glover. *The Color Purple* was released in 1985 to mixed reviews, but Winfrey's performance was praised. One of the critics for *Newsweek* magazine, David Ansen, wrote that Winfrey's performance was a "brazen delight."[3] In *Variety*, a weekly newspaper devoted exclusively to the entertainment industry, a reviewer wrote that the "saving grace of the film are the performances." The reviewer took special note of "Oprah Winfrey's burly Sofia" as an example of fine acting.[4]

But *The Color Purple* also created a tempest of political controversy. Many African-American men felt it portrayed

As a child, Winfrey had dreamed of acting. Quincy Jones gave her the chance.

Winfrey was perfect for the role of Sophia in *The Color Purple*.

them in a purely negative light. Several black journalists criticized the film angrily.

Disgruntled moviegoers made their dissatisfaction known. In Los Angeles, at the film's premiere, dozens of protesters stood outside the theater with picket signs. In Chicago, several hundred African Americans jammed the Progressive Community Church to complain about the way *The Color Purple* negatively portrayed their race.

Winfrey responded to criticism by agreeing that the movie was brutally honest, but she insisted it also had relevance. During an interview with the *Los Angeles Times*, she said, "If this film is going to raise some issues, I'm tired of hearing about what it's doing to the black men. Let's talk about the issue of wife abuse, violence against women, sexual abuse of children in the home." Winfrey added: "What the book did for me and what the movie is doing for other women who are sexually abused, is pointing up that you're not the only one."[5]

Despite the brouhaha, many critics put *The Color Purple* on their year's list of top ten favorites. Ultimately, the film earned a good deal of money and garnered several Academy Award nominations, for everything from costumes to best picture. Winfrey was nominated for best supporting actress,

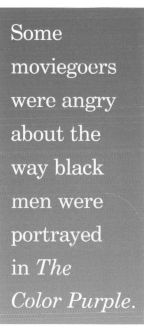

Some moviegoers were angry about the way black men were portrayed in *The Color Purple.*

Winfrey was thrilled to hear that
she was nominated for an Academy Award.

and when she heard the news, she expressed her excitement about her first movie role, saying, "I got the bug!"[6] Despite its many nominations, *The Color Purple* did not win any Oscars.

In 1986 Winfrey had a small role in the film *Native Son*, based on the novel by Richard Wright. Viewers and critics alike were critical of the film. Winfrey's role as the mother of the lead character, Bigger, was not singled out for commendation.

Still, everything seemed to be falling neatly into place in Winfrey's life, even romance. Early in 1986, Winfrey met Stedman Graham, a tall, handsome businessman and founder of the nonprofit organization Athletes Against Drugs. About six months after meeting him, Winfrey was ready to let her fans know she was smitten with the six-foot-six-inch Stedman. "The success of my show is great, losing weight is great, but nothing compares with being in love," she said.[7]

Winfrey was having a very good year indeed. There seemed to be no limit to what she could accomplish. "I want to have a movie career, a television career, a talk-show career. . . . I believe in my own possibilities, and I feel I can do it all."[8]

Chapter 8

Big
Business

efore Oprah Winfrey, only two women in the entertainment industry had owned their own production companies. One was a popular silent-movie actress from the 1930s, Mary Pickford, and the other was comedian and actress Lucille Ball (1911–1989). In 1986 Winfrey became the first black woman in history to open her own studio and produce movies and television shows. She named her new company Harpo, spelling Oprah backward.

Winfrey spent $10 million to buy buildings to house her production company. The complex, not too far from the center of downtown Chicago, takes up an entire square block. The property includes three big studios, an office, screening rooms, even a roomy kitchen. A perfectionist by nature, Winfrey invested another $10 million to have the buildings renovated to her specifications. All the

"Nothing compares with being in love," said Winfrey about her newfound happiness with boyfriend Stedman Graham.

remodeling took time, so Harpo studios did not officially open until two years later.

Meanwhile, Winfrey jumped right into her new role as chief executive. A great lover of books, she decided to buy the rights to literary works so she could eventually turn them into movies. One of the first books she bought was Toni Morrison's novel *Beloved*. Her company also bought the rights to other African-American authors' books, such as *The Wedding* by Dorothy West and *Their Eyes Were Watching God* by Zora Neale Hurston.

The possibilities for the production company appeared limitless. Winfrey had money and tremendous creative inspiration. "It will be as big as we want it to be, depending on what we want to do," she said.[1]

But Winfrey's dream of developing movies never took her away from her devotion to her own television talk show. She continued to pour her energy and heart into each show, and her popularity grew. By May 1987, *The Oprah Winfrey Show* had been on national television for more than nine months, and Winfrey was about to win the first Daytime Emmy Award for Outstanding Talk Show Host.

An Emmy is like an Academy Award, but it recognizes television programs instead of movies. The same year, Winfrey also garnered Emmys for Outstanding Talk Show and Outstanding Talk Show Director.

A beaming Winfrey in 1987 holds the first of many
Daytime Emmys for Outstanding Talk Show Host.

There was another award Winfrey was soon to earn—her college diploma. Deciding it was time to take care of unfinished business, Winfrey re-enrolled at Tennessee State University, finished her senior project, and finally completed the requirements for her college degree. The university asked Winfrey to give the commencement speech on graduation day, when she received her diploma along with rest of the class of 1987.

In her speech, Winfrey announced that she would endow ten scholarships to TSU in honor of her father, Vernon Winfrey. She had never forgotten his emphasis on the importance of education, and the way he had inspired her to work hard and succeed in school. Each scholarship, valued at $77,000, would be awarded on the basis of financial need and academic excellence. All recipients would have to maintain at least a B average in their courses. Winfrey still contributes $25,000 each year to the fund.

Winfrey was able to be generous because she was making solid financial decisions. In 1988, only a year after forming Harpo, Winfrey bought the rights to her own talk show from ABC television. This meant she did not have to answer to anyone else when it came to making decisions about the direction of her show. She could also produce *The Oprah Winfrey Show* in her own studios. Winfrey was now her own boss.

Although Winfrey has a reputation for being a caring and generous boss, she is also known as an executive who expects a lot from her employees. This combination seems to inspire exceptional loyalty from her staff.

"People adore her," explained Dan Santow, a former producer on the show. "They give up their lives for her. . . .[2] Another producer, Mary Kay Clinton, once said, "I would take a bullet for her."[3]

In 1988 Winfrey was also pre-sented with the Broadcaster of the Year Award, given by the International Radio and Television Society. She was the youngest recip-ient of the prestigious award in the society's history.

With support from her hard-working staff, Winfrey was geared up to begin production on a new

> "They give up their lives for her. Everything, all your time and energy is given to Oprah."

project. Winfrey set her sights on a book written by Gloria Naylor. The book, titled *The Women of Brewster Place*, tells the story of seven African-American women who live in a run-down tenement building on Brewster Street, located in a fictional northern town. One of the reasons Winfrey was drawn to this novel was that it showed African-American life in a realistic way.

The Women of Brewster Place portrayed the African-American neighborhood as a thriving place where people cared about their families, looked after their neighbors, and took care of their own property and businesses. Winfrey knew that many white Americans were unaware

Winfrey, center, and the cast of *The Women of Brewster Place*.

that neighborhoods like the fictional Brewster Place really do exist. "The point of having your own company is that you can show that [they do]," she said.[4]

The production for *Brewster Place* began in April 1988. It was broadcast the next year as a four-part miniseries on ABC television. Winfrey had her first starring role as one of the seven women. She played a character named Mattie Michael. Other famous stars in the miniseries included Cicely Tyson and Robin Givens.

Although *Brewster Place* got mixed reviews, it attracted a sizable audience, thanks in part to Winfrey's popularity. Winfrey's fans wanted to see her in a television role other than talk show host. Impressed with the size of the viewing audience, ABC contracted Harpo Productions for thirteen more episodes to be spun off from the original miniseries.

Harpo Productions spent $10 million on the project. But despite the company's financial investment and hard work on the project, the critics panned the series, calling it bland. After only four episodes, ABC canceled the show. Winfrey was disappointed but not disheartened. She looked at the cancellation philosophically. Whether she succeeded or not, she was glad she had tried.[5] Soon after, ABC contracted Harpo Productions to develop four made-for-television movies, with Winfrey starring in two of them.

Food continued to be an issue for Winfrey. At one point she went on a strict diet and lost enough weight to fit into a size 10 jeans. In November 1988, she showed her new body off to her talk show audience, along with a red wagon filled with sixty-seven pounds of animal fat. The audience thundered with applause, but only months later Winfrey had regained the weight and more. For years, her weight fluctuations were frequent fodder for cruel tabloid headlines.

Winfrey's enterprising endeavors expanded to other areas, too. In 1989, not only did Harpo Studios formally open with the renovations completed, but Winfrey also opened a Chicago restaurant called *The Eccentric*. Her partner was Richard Melman, an established restaurateur. The restaurant is no longer in business, but for a time it was a popular Chicago hot spot. *The Eccentric* was unique because it was designed inside a huge factory warehouse and divided into several sections, each with cuisine from a different country.

The year 1989 continued with stark peaks and valleys. Morehouse College in Atlanta, Georgia, bestowed an honorary doctorate on Winfrey. Impressed with the programs at the college, Winfrey established the Oprah Winfrey Endowment Scholarship Fund to provide tuition payments for academically promising students who were in need of financial assistance. She donated an initial $1 million to the fund.

She looked slim and smug in her new size 10 jeans—
but this would not be the end of Winfrey's battle with the bulge.

◆ ◆ ◆ ◆ ◆

The year closed out with sad news. Only three days before Christmas 1989, Winfrey's half-brother, Jeffrey Lee, died from AIDS. Winfrey read a formal statement to the press. "My family, like thousands of others throughout the world, grieves not just for the death of one young man, but for the many unfulfilled dreams and accomplishments that society has been denied because of AIDS."[6]

Chapter 9

Subject Matters

It was 1990, the launch not only of a new decade but also a leap into new territory on Winfrey's talk show. During a taping, Winfrey was interviewing a woman who was a victim of child abuse. Suddenly, Winfrey's own tragic experiences years ago came flashing in front of her. Gripped with emotion, she tearfully revealed her childhood abuse to audiences all over the world.

This was a turning point for Winfrey. For years, she had tried to hide her past from the public. Now she realized that by telling her personal story, she might help other young victims to speak out, gain power, and, she hoped, stop their own abuse. "A part of my mission in life now is to encourage every other child who has been abused to tell," Winfrey said. "You tell, and if they don't believe you, you keep telling. You tell everybody until somebody listens to you."[1]

From that moment forward, Winfrey began using her influence to help victims of child abuse. A year later, on November 1, 1991, Winfrey was in Washington, D.C., standing before members of the United States Senate Judiciary Committee and describing her personal, heart-wrenching story of child abuse. She wanted to give her support to the passage of the National Childhood Protection Act. "You lose your childhood when you've been abused," she told the committee.[2]

If the law passed, it would mean that people who work with children could check a national database of convicted abusers and make sure they did not hire anyone with a history of hurting children.

At first, the law did not pass. But two years later, in December 1993, President Bill Clinton signed the National Child Protection Act into law. It was nicknamed the "Oprah bill," and Winfrey stood next to the president during the historic signing ceremony in the White House.

Winfrey continued to keep her focus on children. Also in 1991, her company started producing after-school specials with ABC that dealt with teen issues like drugs and self-esteem. She also produced a prime-time movie called *Scared Silent: Exposing and Ending Child Abuse*. This was a very personal project for Winfrey, and she introduced the

By speaking out, Winfrey wanted to protect other children
from the trauma of abuse that she had suffered as a child.

movie herself saying, "I'm Oprah Winfrey, and like millions of other Americans, I'm a survivor of child abuse."

Meanwhile, Winfrey continued to battle with her weight. On the day she accepted her third Daytime Emmy Award for Outstanding Talk Show Host in 1992, Winfrey had reached her highest weight yet—237 pounds. She said later that rather than feeling happy during the ceremony and basking in the honor, she was mortified. "I felt like such a loser, like I'd lost control of my life," she said. "I was the fattest woman in the room."[3]

Once again, Winfrey was determined to kick her habit of overeating. Soon after the Emmy Award show, Winfrey checked herself into a spa for weight reduction in Telluride, Colorado. It was there that she met personal trainer Bob Greene.

He was the first person to really help Winfrey make the connection between her emotions and food. Winfrey learned that whenever she felt nervous, fearful, or stressed out she would reach for food to calm herself down. "I'd think: 'I gotta eat. I gotta eat. I gotta eat.' Then I'd feel calmer."[4] By 1993 she had gotten her weight down to 150 pounds.

Greene has remained Winfrey's diet and fitness guru. Even now, she looks to Greene for personal diet advice and inspiration. They work so well as a team that Winfrey has co-authored best-selling books with Greene. Their first collaboration, titled *Make the Connection: Ten Steps to*

Once Winfrey started working out, she was fit enough to participate in fund-raisers like this run for cancer research.

a Better Body and a Better Life, sold more than 2 million copies.

Another way Greene helped Winfrey "make the connection" was by tapping into her competitive nature. With Greene's guidance and encouragement, Winfrey was able to up her regular jogging routine to at least eight miles a day. "If Bob wants to push me [when I'm running], he'll say 'See that woman in the pink suit? You can take her,' And I'll kill myself to run past her."[5]

In fact, Winfrey was feeling so positive and powerful about her life that when Stedman asked her to marry him in November 1992, she accepted. The couple set a date for the following September for their wedding.

That was not the only project they joined hands in. Around the same time, Winfrey starred as LaJoe Rivers in *There Are No Children Here*, an ABC television movie about life in a Chicago housing project. She donated the $500,000 she earned for the film to set up a charity called Families for a Better Life. Her fiancé, Stedman Graham, co-founded the charity.

The same year Winfrey announced she would be writing her autobiography with writer Joan Barthel. Fans waited in anticipation. Then, in 1993, she disappointed them by announcing the book's cancellation. Winfrey explained: "I'm in the heart of a learning curve. I feel there are important discoveries yet to be made."[6]

Instead, Winfrey worked on a cookbook of low-fat recipes with her personal chef Rosie Daley. It was titled *In the Kitchen with Rosie: Oprah's Favorite Recipes*. Winfrey promoted the book, published in 1994, on her talk show, and it immediately became a runaway best-seller. In its first four years, the cookbook sold more than 6 million copies.[7]

Winfrey continued to be in a

> "I'm in the heart of a learning curve. I feel there are important discoveries yet to be made."

committed relationship with Stedman Graham, but it did not take long before their wedding plans were called off. The media was ablaze with speculation about why the couple's nuptials were not going to take place.

Winfrey explained the change of plans this way: "There was a time in my life when I needed marriage to validate myself, but now I'm content with what my relationship gives me." Then she added, "I'm very sorry I ever mentioned Stedman's name to the press. The whole wedding thing might not be such a big issue if I had never mentioned it."[8]

Winfrey also went public with her decision not to have children. She did not want to make the mistakes that were made during her own childhood. Speaking of motherhood, she said, "I always felt that I don't even know how to do that."[9]

Also during 1994, Winfrey was inducted into the Academy of Television Arts and Sciences Hall of Fame. This is one of the highest honors an entertainer can receive, but initially Winfrey turned it down. She felt there were other entertainers who deserved the award more. But in the end, Winfrey accepted the award graciously as one of the most important honors of her life.

At the end of her 1994 talk show season, Winfrey made an important decision. By then, television featured a variety of talk shows, and many—including Winfrey's— often focused on sensationalism and "trash" topics.

Winfrey had tried to maintain her standards, but she knew that her program was contributing to the trend. "I am embarrassed by how far over the line [talk show] topics have gone, but I also recognize my own contribution to this," she said. "People should not be surprised and humiliated on national television for the purpose of entertainment. I was ashamed of myself."[10] She promised to do more uplifting shows, with positive role models that would "strengthen the human spirit."[11]

To help other women achieve their potential, in 1995 Winfrey donated $1 million to Spelman College in Atlanta, Georgia, a school attended primarily by African-American women. Winfrey directed the money to be used in the sciences, specifically for research in environmental biology and chemistry.[12] She also financed the college education of one thousand African-American men at Morehouse College, in Atlanta, Georgia, pledging $12 million to the institution.

Winfrey's donations were helping people achieve higher education, but the power of her television show could also enrich the minds of her viewers. Her interest in bringing literature into the homes of her audience had not dimmed. In September 1996, she made an on-air commitment to share her love of books. Winfrey decided to encourage her audience to read by introducing an on-air reading group, which she named "Oprah's Book Club."

Winfrey loves to read, and her millions of fans race out to buy any book she praises. These are just a few of her early book-club selections.

Once each month, Winfrey recommended a book to her audience. A month later, the author of the selected novel appeared as a guest on the talk show. Winfrey's first selection was *The Deep End of the Ocean*, by Jacquelyn Mitchard. It tells the dramatic story of a child's disappearance and the shattering effects it has on the family.

Oprah's book club was a tremendous success. Every book Winfrey selected became an instant hit, and sales skyrocketed. Talking about books became so popular that people in cities and towns all over the country started forming their own book groups.

Another subject Winfrey discussed on her talk show created a big stir. But this time, the publicity was not glowing. In 1996 the public was first made aware of Mad Cow Disease. It is a rare sickness carried by infected cows. At the time, the only sick cows were found in England, and herds of cattle there were slaughtered to prevent the disease from spreading. One day, when Winfrey had a guest on her show talking about the problem, she blurted out, "It has just stopped me from eating another burger!"[13]

Winfrey followed with another show to try to quell the hoopla over her remark. Guests on the program were Dr. Gary Weber of the National Cattlemen's Beef Association and Iowa cattle rancher Connie Greig. They both assured viewers that the cattle industry was protecting people and producing safe food.

It did not matter. Texas cattlemen were angry. They accused Winfrey of causing such a panic that people were no longer buying beef—and they filed a lawsuit against her, demanding $12 million in damages.

Winfrey had to appear in a Texas courtroom to fight the charges. She saw it as a case against her right to free speech. "I come from a people who struggled and died to use their voice in this country and I refuse to be muzzled," she said.[14]

Winfrey took her talk show to Texas. While the month-long trial was going on, her production staff worked hard

Did Winfrey's offhand remark stop Americans from buying beef?
"Not guilty!" said the jury.

to produce programs from there. Several of the shows showcased Texas lifestyles with sprawling mansions and huge hairdos. She also invited Texas celebrities onto the show, including actor Patrick Swayze and country singer Clint Black.

Ultimately, Winfrey was found innocent of causing a crash in the meat market. Outside the courthouse, Winfrey thrust her fists up in victory and shouted tearfully, "Yes! Free speech not only lives, it rocks."[15]

With the controversy finally put to rest, Winfrey had energy left to burn. She flew back to Chicago, ready to let her influence spread in new directions.

Chapter 10

In Her Prime Time

infrey had a new plan. She wanted to encourage her audience to give to charity. On September 18, 1997, she introduced Oprah's Angel Network, devising a way for viewers all over the country to contribute to worthy causes by sending in their spare change. She called it "The World's Largest Piggy Bank." The Angel Network collected viewers' coins, dollars, and checks and set up a scholarship fund to help needy students pay for their college tuition. The first year alone, the Angel Network brought in over $3 million. By October 2004, it had raised nearly 20 million for more than one hundred charities.[1]

Another initial project the Angel Network sponsored was an organization called Habitat for Humanity. This charity became famous when former president Jimmy Carter and his wife, Rosalynn, volunteered some of their

Habitat for Humanity

In 1976, millionaires Millard and Linda Fuller founded Habitat for Humanity, a Christian-based nonprofit organization. The purpose of this international agency is to build low-cost but quality housing for people who need a place to live. All the houses are built by volunteers. The homes are sold at no profit, and if mortgage loans are needed, no interest is charged. By 2003, Habitat had built more than one hundred thousand homes overseas in ninety-two countries. By 2005, housing for more than one million people worldwide will be provided by building projects sponsored by Habitat for Humanity. Homeowners are usually expected to put in at least five hundred hours working on their own houses or on another project sponsored by the organization.

time to help build homes for low-income families. Habitat for Humanity also provides interest-free mortgages for families in exchange for construction they do on their future homes. Winfrey's goal was to build two hundred homes throughout the country. She donated an initial $55,000 and encouraged businesses and viewers to contribute as well.

The public was keenly aware of Winfrey's altruistic endeavors. In a survey taken around the same time the

IN HER PRIME TIME

Angel Network was organized—and reported in *U.S. News and World Report*—Winfrey ranked second only to Mother Teresa in a poll asking people to name who was more likely to go to heaven.[2]

This was quite an honor because Mother Teresa, who died in 1997, was a world-famous Catholic nun who had worked among the poor of Calcutta, India. Mother Teresa won a Noble Peace Prize, and Pope John Paul II beatified her—which means he gave her the extraordinary honor of sainthood.

Winfrey won admiration for her good deeds, but she remained steadfastly focused on business interests as well. This allowed her to give generously to projects she believed in. According to a 1998 article in *Forbes* magazine, a popular business publication, Winfrey was ranked as one of the wealthiest women in entertainment. The editors estimated Winfrey's annual income at the time to be about $125 million. By 2003, her net worth was estimated at more than $1 billion, making her the first African-American woman listed in *Forbes* annual tally of billionaires.[3]

The same year the Angel Network took flight, Winfrey finished a movie that had taken almost a decade to produce. It was called *Beloved*, based on the Pulitzer Prize–winning novel of the same name by Toni Morrison.

The author, a famous African-American fiction writer and poet, was also one of Winfrey's mentors. Ever since

Winfrey had first read the book, she knew she wanted to make it into a film. "*Beloved* is my passion. . . . This is the fulfillment of a lifelong dream for me," Winfrey said.[4]

Jonathan Demme directed the movie. Winfrey played Sethe, a slave who had escaped in 1837 from the Sweet Home Plantation. In the film, Sethe leaves her daughter behind but is forever haunted by memories of her. She also meets another former slave from the plantation, Paul D., who is played by the actor Danny Glover.

Winfrey with *Beloved* costars Thandie Newton, left, and Kimberly Elise, right. For Winfrey, making this movie was "the fulfillment of a lifelong dream."

Winfrey found working on the film about slaves to be emotionally draining because rather than just imagining what it would be like to be a slave, she actually started to experience it. "You can talk about it on an intellectual level, but during the process of doing *Beloved*, for the first time, I went to the knowing place," she said.[5]

Beloved was a movie Winfrey cherished, and her acting received glowing reviews by critics. A reviewer from the music magazine *Rolling Stone* called Winfrey's portrayal of Sethe "pitch-perfect."[6]

Despite all the praise for Winfrey's performance, the movie did not do well at the box office. Some critics suspected that the reason people stayed away from the theaters was that the subject of slavery was too emotionally charged for audiences to handle.

Winfrey was disappointed but not devastated. She threw her energies into another project, changing the direction of her talk show. At the start of the 1998 television season, she named the new focus of her show "Change Your Life TV." From that time forward, Winfrey planned her segments around encouraging viewers to make positive changes in their lives.

In September 1999, Winfrey and her boyfriend Stedman Graham co-taught a course called Dynamics of Leadership at the J. L. Kellogg Graduate School of Management at Northwestern University. The classes, held one night a week for ten weeks, taught students how they could develop their own leadership and management skills. Not surprisingly, the course was well attended and was offered again the following fall.

The assistant dean of the school, Rich Honack, said that the students had given Winfrey "reviews that were among the strongest of any professor." But Winfrey was more critical of herself, saying, "I gave myself a B and I'm coming back to get an A because I now know how to get it."[7]

Meanwhile, the tabloids continued to hound the couple about their wedding plans. Finally, Winfrey said flatly, "Neither of us is ready to get married."[8]

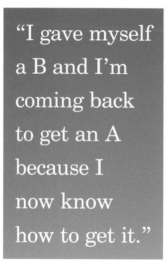

"I gave myself a B and I'm coming back to get an A because I now know how to get it."

But Winfrey was always ready to suggest a good book to her audience. In November 1999, Winfrey was awarded the National Book Foundation's 50th Anniversary Gold Medal because she had made a commitment to inspire millions of people to read.

Within the next couple of years, Winfrey made another commitment. She joined forces with the media moguls Geraldine Laybourne and the principals of the Carsey-Werner-Mandabach Company to start a women's cable network called Oxygen. It was launched in February 2000 and was linked simultaneously to Winfrey's already popular Website <http://www.oprah.com>.

The first program Winfrey produced for Oxygen was

Winfrey's tremendous contribution to reading
and books earned her this special trophy.

Helping people is Winfrey's mission, from "Change Your Life TV" to interactive workshops like this "Live Your Best Life Tour" in Seattle.

◆ ◆ ◆ ◆ ◆

Oprah Goes Online. It was a twelve-part series offering a step-by-step exploration of the Internet. The programs were co-hosted by her good friend Gayle King. Millions of women all over the country tuned in and learned first-hand how to connect to the Internet and go online.

But Winfrey did not stop there. The year 2000 continued to be a monumental one.

Chapter 11

More on
the Horizon

In April 2000, Winfrey launched the most successful magazine start-up in publishing history. She named her magazine, which was a joint venture with Hearst magazines, *O—The Oprah Magazine.* When discussing why she chose the one-letter name for her publication, she said, "What I like about *O*, is that it is simple and direct, and it is what a lot of my friends call me."[1]

Winfrey once again looked for help from her friend Gayle King, naming her executive editor of the magazine. However, Winfrey still oversaw even minor details of the publication. Controversial reports from the magazine industry swirled around, claiming Winfrey was too controlling and making staffers uneasy. In response, Winfrey said, "I wasn't too controlling. I needed to be involved. When you get me, you are not getting an image. You are

"*O* is what a lot of my friends call me," said Winfrey
as she launched her new magazine.

not getting a figurehead. You're not getting a theme song. You're getting all of me."[2]

O—The Oprah Magazine sold out its premier issue. It continued to build momentum, and today the magazine has more than 2 million regular readers. Unlike other women's magazines, which often focus on simplistic answers to serious issues, Winfrey oversees editorial content to make sure topics are covered with the same sensitivity and depth she offers on her daily talk show. Winfrey also continues to write a column each month and is photographed for each of *O*'s covers.

In April 2002, Winfrey announced that she was taking a break from her monthly book club. "I will continue featuring books on *The Oprah Winfrey Show* when I feel they merit my heartfelt recommendation," she said.[3]

Winfrey continued to focus her daily talk show on topics that were relevant to her viewers. Several of her guests were psychologists and authors who offered her audience ways they could improve their lives. Among them was the psychologist Dr. Phil McGraw, who soon became a favorite guest as a result of his "tell it like it is" style.

Thanks to regular Oprah spots, Dr. Phil began hosting his own spin-off daytime show, *Dr. Phil*, premiering in September 2002. It is produced by Winfrey's Harpo Productions in collaboration with Paramount Television. "It was her vision about me and what I could do that put me in the direction I've taken with my life . . . ," McGraw said. "She's just a great resource, a great mentor . . . and I'm lucky to say, a very good and dear friend."[4]

As Winfrey neared her fiftieth year, she let the public know she was going to do it in style. In the October 2003 issue of *O* magazine, Winfrey wrote, "I'm ready to claim this next decade for all it's worth and take it to the max. I intend to stretch myself and rock so hard with the 50s that by the time I'm through, everybody I know is going to wish they were 50-something, or at least 49 and waiting to be."[5]

The Controversy Around Dr. Phil

As a television psychologist, Dr. Phillip C. McGraw, who pulls in 5 million viewers a day, is a controversial figure. The format of his television program is advice-driven, but some critics charge that his approach is too negative and "in-your-face." On more than one occasion, McGraw, in his native Texas drawl, has said to a guest seated on his stage, "You're an idiot!" McGraw has said that his methods are a way to encourage people to "get real."[6] Professionals in the field have accused him of not taking into account psychological reasons for people's behavior, such as depression or neuroses. "I'm not for everybody," he says.[7] Still, Dr. Phil's books have become bestsellers and include these titles: *Family First, Getting Real, Life Strategies, Self Matter,* and *The Ultimate Weight Solution.*

The no-nonsense Dr. Phil freely scolds his viewers
for being "too fat" or "bad parents."

> "I'm ready to claim this next decade for all it's worth and take it to the max."

Winfrey was true to her word. The celebration began on Thursday, January 29, 2004, with a special live edition of her TV show filled with surprises her staff had kept from her for weeks. "We banned her from her own building. We said, 'Stay home you can't come in,'" said Ellen Rakieten, executive producer of Winfrey's talk show.[8]

Winfrey's friend Gayle King and the actor John Travolta hosted the star-studded program. Special guests included the singers Tina Turner and Stevie Wonder, and the talk show host Jay Leno. Former president of South Africa Nelson Mandela, Nobel Peace Prize–winner Desmond Tutu, actors Tom Cruise, Julia Roberts, Jennifer Lopez, and Jennifer Aniston, as well as music mogul producer Quincy Jones and movie producer Steven Spielberg sent special birthday wishes via satellite.

In addition, a group of South African children whom she had visited and taken under her wing sang birthday wishes, addressing Winfrey as "Mama Oprah." Actor Sidney Poitier toasted Winfrey and spoke about her commitment to change lives for the better all over the world.

Winfrey was also presented with a four-hundred-pound birthday cake decorated with hand-painted portraits of her. But the lavish celebration was just the beginning. The next day there was an all-women luncheon with fifty of

Winfrey's friends in attendance at the Bel Air Hotel, in Los Angeles, California.

On Saturday evening, Winfrey was the guest of honor at a black-tie party hosted by her neighbors in Montecito, California. More than two hundred celebrity guests attended, including Arnold Schwarzenegger and Madonna. Dinner was served on special apple-green china and crystal created just for Winfrey. There were more than one hundred thousand orchids decorating the area and a clear dance floor built over a swimming pool just for the occasion. The opulent bash cost several million dollars.

After Winfrey's over-the-top birthday celebration, she considered ways to give her studio audience its own special treat. She found one.

On Monday, September 13, 2004, during the premiere show of Winfrey's nineteenth season, she asked eleven people from the audience to come up on stage. She handed each one keys to a Pontiac G-6 car, worth $28,000 and donated by General Motors.

That was not all. Next, gift boxes were handed out to each person in the audience. Winfrey said *someone* has keys to a twelfth car in their gift box. Then Winfrey suddenly shouted: "Everybody gets a car! Everybody gets a car! Everybody gets a car!"[9] Winfrey started jumping up and down, and the thrilled studio audience broke into pandemonium.

The audience members had been chosen because either they or someone in their family had written to the show about needing a new car. Afterward, some people said it was not a real giveaway because everyone who got a car had to pay up to $7,000 in taxes. The new car owners had a choice of giving the car back, keeping it and paying the taxes, or selling the new cars and keeping the profit.[10]

Cars were not the only gifts Winfrey gave away that day. She also gave a young woman who had spent her life in foster care and homeless shelters a $10,000 wardrobe and a four-year college scholarship.

Winfrey also continues to give her all when it comes to encouraging people to read. She challenged her audience in 2004 when she revived Oprah's Book Club with the eight-hundred-plus-page classic novel *Anna Karenina* by Leo Tolstoy, followed by the shorter twentieth-century novel *The Heart Is a Lonely Hunter* by Carson McCullers.

Winfrey sets her standards high, whether she is reporting, acting, producing, publishing a magazine, running a media company, hosting her talk show, or donating more than $50 million to charities. And she encourages countless others to make the most of their lives, too. Oprah Winfrey has proved that no matter what hardships present themselves, with an open heart, a fierce, positive spirit, and bountiful energy—life's possibilities are limitless.

When Oprah Winfrey talks, people listen.

Chronology

1954—Oprah Winfrey is born in Kosciusko, Mississippi, on January 29.

1958—Oprah's mother, Vernita Lee, moves to Milwaukee, Wisconsin. Her grandmother raises her.

1960—Moves to Milwaukee to live with her mother.

1968—Moves to Nashville, Tennessee, to live with her father, Vernon Winfrey.

1971—Radio station WVOL hires her part-time to read the news; graduates from Nashville's East High School and goes to Tennessee State University.

1972—Is crowned Miss Black Nashville and Miss Black Tennessee.

1973—Becomes the first African-American woman to co-anchor the news on Nashville's WTVF-TV.

1976—Hired by WJZ-TV in Baltimore to co-anchor the local news.

1977—WJZ-TV asks her to co-host *People Are Talking* with Richard Sher.

1984—WLS-TV in Chicago hires her to host *A.M. Chicago*.

1985—*A.M. Chicago* becomes *The Oprah Winfrey Show*; she is cast as Sofia in *The Color Purple*.

1986—Nominated for an Academy Award as Best Supporting Actress for her role in *The Color Purple*; national syndication of *The Oprah Winfrey Show*; establishes her own production company.

1987—Goes back to finish school at Tennessee State University; *The Oprah Winfrey Show* receives several Emmy awards, including Winfrey's first for Outstanding Talk Show Host.

1988—Named Broadcaster of the Year by the International Television and Radio Society; produces and stars in a miniseries *The Women of Brewster Place*; establishes Harpo Studios in Chicago; assumes ownership of her show.

1989—Awarded an honorary doctorate by Morehouse College; half brother, Jeffrey Lee, dies.

1991—Appears before Congress in support of the National Child Protection Act.

1993—The National Child Protection Act is signed into law, and becomes known as the "Oprah bill."

1994—Wins Best Talk Show and Best Talk Show Host at the Daytime Emmy Awards; *In the Kitchen with Rosie: Oprah's Favorite Recipes* is published.

CHRONOLOGY

1995—Is the only entertainer and the only African American on *Forbes* magazine's list of 400 richest Americans.

1996— Launches Oprah's Book Club.

1997—Starts charity organization Oprah's Angel Network.

1998—Receives a Lifetime Achievement Award from the Daytime Emmy Awards; produces and stars in the film *Beloved*.

2000—Supports Oxygen Media, a women's cable-television network; with Hearst Publications she launches *O—The Oprah Magazine*.

2002—Breaks ground for the Oprah Winfrey Leadership Academy for Girls in South Africa, to which she contributes $10 million.

2003—Is honored with the Marian Anderson Award for artistic and humanitarian achievement.

2004—Celebrates the opening of the nineteenth season of *The Oprah Winfrey Show* by giving every one of the 276 people in her audience a new car.

2004—Hosts, with actor Tom Cruise, the Nobel Peace Prize Concert in Oslo, Norway.

Chapter Notes

Chapter 1. "Okay, God, I Get It!"

1. "Christmas Kindness: South Africa 2002,"
© 2004 Harpo Productions, Inc., <http://www.oprah.com/presents/2003/christmaskindness/leadership/pres_2003_ck_leadership.jhtml> (October 25, 2004).

2. Ibid.

3. Ibid.

4. "Oprah's Revelation, December 17, 2003,"
© 2004 Paramount Pictures, <http://et.tv.yahoo.com/tv/2003/12/17/oprah_primetime/> (October 25, 2004).

5. Ibid.

6. "Oprah Winfrey Hosts HOPE *worldwide* Party in Soweto," © 2001 HOPE *worldwide*, <http://hopeww.org/home/2002/12/oprah.htm> (October 25, 2004).

7. Ibid.

8. Tanya Barrientos and Annette John-Hall, "Oprah's Here, Honored for Her Heart," © 2003 *The Inquirer* (Philadelphia), <http://www.philly.com/mld/philly/entertainment/7288640.htm> (October 25, 2004).

Chapter 2. Born Into Hardship

1. Robert Waldron, *Oprah!* (New York: St. Martin's Press, 1987), p. 11.

2. Ibid., pp. 12, 17.

3. Norman King, *Everybody Loves Oprah! Her Remarkable Life Story* (New York: William Morrow and Company, 1987), p. 30.

CHAPTER NOTES

4. Alan Richman, "Oprah," *People Weekly*, January 12, 1987, p. 50.

5. Bill Adler, ed., *The Uncommon Wisdom of Oprah Winfrey* (Secaucus, N.J.: Birch Lane Press, 1997), p. 4.

6. Waldron, p. 20.

7. Ibid., p. 14.

8. Richman, p. 50.

9. John Culhane, "Oprah Winfrey: How Truth Changed Her Life," *Reader's Digest*, February 1989, p. 102.

Chapter 3. Tough Times

1. Bill Adler, ed., *The Uncommon Wisdom of Oprah Winfrey* (Secaucus, N.J.: Birch Lane Press, 1997), p. 8.

2. Sugar Rautbord, "Oprah Winfrey," *Interview* magazine, March 1986, p. 62.

3. Marilyn Johnson and Dana Fineman, "Oprah Winfrey: A Life in Books," *Life*, September 1997, p. 9.

4. Adler, p. 10.

5. Joanna Powell, "I Was Trying to Fill Something Deeper," *Good Housekeeping*, October 1996, p. 82.

6. Joan Barthel, "Oprah," *Ms.*, August 1986, p. 56.

7. Robert Waldron, *Oprah!* (New York: St. Martin's Press, 1987), p. 29.

8. Adler, p. 16.

Chapter 4. Beating the Odds

1. Marilyn Johnson and Dana Fineman, "Oprah Winfrey: A Life in Books," *Life*, September 1997.

2. Janet Lowe, *Oprah Winfrey Speaks* (New York: John Wiley & Sons, Inc., 1998), p. 14.

3. Norman King, *Everybody Loves Oprah! Her Remarkable Life Story* (New York: William Morrow and Company, 1987), pp. 57–58.

4. Bill Adler, ed., *The Uncommon Wisdom of Oprah Winfrey* (Secaucus, N.J.: Birch Lane Press, 1997), p. 29.

5. John Culhane, "Oprah Winfrey: How Truth Changed Her Life," *Reader's Digest*, February 1989, p. 103.

6. Lowe, p. 15.

7. "Oprah Winfrey Interview, February 1991," © Academy of Achievement, Museum of Living History, <http://www.achievement.org/autodoc/page/win0int-2> (October 25, 2004).

8. Ibid.

9. Lowe, p. 29.

10. Adler, p. 33.

Chapter 5. Changing Channels

1. From Winfrey's commencement address at Wellesley College, May 30, 1997.

2. Norman King, *Everybody Loves Oprah! Her Remarkable Life Story* (New York: William Morrow and Company, 1987), p. 79.

3. Robert Waldron, *Oprah!* (New York: St. Martin's Press, 1987), p. 68.

4. "Oprah Winfrey Interview, February 1991," © Academy of Achievement, Museum of Living History, <http://www.achievement.org/autodoc/page/win0int-1> (October 25, 2004).

5. Ibid.

6. Janet Lowe, *Oprah Winfrey Speaks* (New York: John Wiley & Sons, Inc., 1998), p. 43.

7. Ibid.

CHAPTER NOTES

8. Chris Anderson, "Meet Oprah Winfrey," *Good Housekeeping*, August 1986, p. 37.

9. Eric Sherman, "Oprah Winfrey's Success Story," *Ladies' Home Journal*, March 1997, p. 64.

10. Lowe, p. 90.

11. Bill Adler, ed., *The Uncommon Wisdom of Oprah Winfrey* (Secaucus, N.J.: Birch Lane Press, 1997), p. 163.

Chapter 6. In Her Own Name

1. Robert Waldron, *Oprah!* (New York: St. Martin's Press, 1987), p. 78.

2. Ibid., p. 83.

3. George Mair, *Oprah Winfrey: The Real Story* (Secaucus, N.J.: Birch Lane Press, 1994), p. 74.

4. Bill Adler, ed., *The Uncommon Wisdom of Oprah Winfrey* (Secaucus, N.J.: Birch Lane Press, 1997), p. 52.

5. Ibid.

6. Richard Zoglin, "People Sense the Realness," *Time*, September 15, 1986, p. 99.

7. "Big Gain, No Pain," *People*, January 14, 1991, p. 82.

Chapter 7. A Passion for Purple

1. "NOW Honors Oprah for *The Color Purple* Role" *Jet*, June 30, 1986.

2. Bill Adler, ed., *The Uncommon Wisdom of Oprah Winfrey* (Secaucus, N.J.: Birch Lane Press, 1997), p. 238.

3. David Ansen, "We Shall Overcome," *Newsweek*, December 30, 1985, p. 60.

4. "The Color Purple" (review), *Variety*, December 18, 1985.

5. Jack Mathews, "Three 'Color Purple' Actresses Talk About Its Impact," *Los Angeles Times*, January 31, 1986.

6. Janet Lowe, *Oprah Winfrey Speaks* (New York: John Wiley & Sons, Inc., 1998), p. 56.

7. Eric Sherman, "Oprah Winfrey's Success Story," *Ladies' Home Journal*, March 1987, p. 64.

8. George Mair, *Oprah Winfrey: The Real Story* (Secaucus, N.J.: Birch Lane Press, 1994), p. 94.

Chapter 8. Big Business

1. Paul Noglows, "Oprah: The Year of Living Dangerously," *Working Woman*, May 1994, p. 52.

2. "The Oprah Myth," *TV Guide*, January 7, 1995, p. 15.

3. Jackie Rodgers, "Understanding Oprah," *Redbook*, September 1993, p. 134.

4. Susan Letwin, "Oprah Opens Up," *TV Guide*, May 5, 1990, p. 5.

5. Janet Lowe, *Oprah Winfrey Speaks* (New York: John Wiley & Sons, Inc., 1998), p. 110.

6. Bill Adler, ed., *The Uncommon Wisdom of Oprah Winfrey* (Secaucus, N.J.: Birch Lane Press, 1997), p. 266.

Chapter 9. Subject Matters

1. "Oprah Winfrey Interview, February 1991," © Academy of Achievement, Museum of Living History, <http://www.achievement.org/autodoc/page/win0int-1> (October 25, 2004).

2. Mary H. J. Farrell, "Oprah's Crusade," *People Weekly*, December 2, 1991, p. 69.

3. Joanna Powell, "I Was Trying to Fill Something Deeper," *Good Housekeeping*, October 1996, p. 80.

CHAPTER NOTES

—◊◊◊—

4. Ibid.

5. Dana Kennedy, "Oprah, Act Two," *Entertainment Weekly*, September 9, 1994, p. 20.

6. "Oprah Winfrey" *People Weekly*, December 27, 1993, p. 52.

7. Janet Lowe, *Oprah Winfrey Speaks* (New York: John Wiley & Sons, Inc., 1998), p. 155.

8. Bill Adler, ed., *The Uncommon Wisdom of Oprah Winfrey* (Secaucus, N.J.: Birch Lane Press, 1997), p. 210.

9. "How Oprah Conquered the US," BBC News, © 2002 <http://news.bbc.co.uk/1/hi/entertainment/tv_and_radio/1868498.stm> (October 25, 2004).

10. Oprah Winfrey, "What We All Can Do to Change TV," *TV Guide*, November 11, 1995, pp. 15–16.

11. Ibid.

12. "Oprah Gives $1 Million to Spelman College's Science Fund," *Jet*, November 27, 1995, p. 10.

13. Barbara Laker and Theresa Conroy, "Cattle Ranchers Should've Known: Oprah Just Doesn't Lose," *San Diego Union Tribune*, March 6, 1998, p. E3.

14. Mark Babineck, Associated Press, February 26, 1998.

15. Aaron Brown, "Oprah Winfrey Verdict," *Good Morning America*, ABC-TV broadcast, February 27, 1998.

Chapter 10. In Her Prime Time

1. Mary Elizabeth Williams, "In Oprah We Trust," *TV Guide*, October 10, 2004.

2. "Oprah a Heavenly Body?" *U.S. News and World Report*, March 31, 1997, p. 18.

3. *People Weekly*, February 2, 2004, p. 52.

4. Bill Adler, ed., *The Uncommon Wisdom of Oprah* (Secaucus, N.J.: Birch Lane Press, 1997), pp. 158–159.

5. Oprah Winfrey and Pearl Cleage, "The Courage to Dream!" *Essence*, December 1998, p. 80.

6. Peter Travers, review of *Beloved*, 1998, © 2004 Rolling Stone, <http://www.rollingstone.com/reviews/movie/_/id/5947279?> (October 25, 2004).

7. Kellogg School of Management, Northwestern University Press Release, January 16, 2000.

8. Adler, pp. 207–212.

Chapter 11. More on the Horizon

1. "New Oprah Magazine Named: O, the Oprah Magazine," *Business Wire*, January 12, 2000, p. 1372.

2. Lynette Clemetson, "It Is Constant Work," *Newsweek*, January 8, 2001.

3. Bridget Kinsella, "Oprah Ends Monthly Book Club," *Publisher's Weekly*, April 8, 2002.

4. *Television Week*, April 19, 2004, p. S4.

5. From *O* magazine, October 2003, quoted in "Oprah Turning 50 with Fire," September 10, 2003, © 2004 Paramount Pictures, <http://et.tv.yahoo.com/tv/2004/01/30/oprahbirthday/> (October 25, 2004).

6. Alene Weintraub, "Getting Real—And Getting Real Rich: Dr. Phil Inc. Keeps Growing, But the Relentless Self-promoter Has His Critics," *Business Week*, June 21, 2004, <http://www.businessweek.com/magazine/content/04_25/b3888088.htm> (October 29, 2004).

7. Ibid.

8. "Oprah's Birthday Weekend," January 29, 2004, © 2004 Paramount Pictures, <http://et.tv.yahoo.com/tv/2004/01/29/oprahbirthday/> (October 25, 2004).

9. "Oprah Winfrey Gives Cars to Audience," September 13, 2004, © Associated Press, <http://apnews.

myway.com/article/20040913/D852SP380.html>
(October 25, 2004).

    10. "Oprah Car Winners Hit With Hefty Tax,"
September 22, 2004, Cable News Network, <http://
money.cnn.com/2004/09/22/news/newsmakers/
oprah_car_tax?cnn=yes> (October 20, 2004).

    11. Ibid.

Further Reading

Blashfield, Jean F. *Oprah Winfrey*. Milwaukee, Wisc.: World Almanac Library, 2003.

Friedrich, Belinda. *Oprah Winfrey*. Philadelphia, Pa.: Chelsea House Publishers, 2001.

Helen S. Garson. *Oprah Winfrey: A Biography*. Westport, Conn.: Greenwood Publishing Group, 2004.

Krohn, Katherine E., and Martha Cosgrove. *Oprah Winfrey*. Minneapolis, Minn.: Lerner Publications Company, 2004.

Presnall, Judith Janda. *Oprah Winfrey*. San Diego, Calif.: Lucent Books, 1999.

Stone, Tanya Lee. *Oprah Winfrey*. Brookfield, Conn.: Millbrook Press, 2001.

Internet Addresses

Oprah's Official Web site
    <http://www.oprah.com>

Links to lots of articles and Web sites about Oprah
    <http://www.sirlinksalot.net/oprah.html>

Academy of Achievement, a Museum of Living
    History, The Hall of Business
    <http://www.achievement.org/autodoc/page/
    win0bio-1>

The Internet Movie Database has an Oprah Winfrey
    filmography, with links to more information
    about her movies.
    <http://www.imdb.com/name/nm0001856>

Index

Page numbers for photographs are in **boldface** type.

INDEX